What kinds of coverings do animals have?

Bobbie Kalman

🌳 Crabtree Publishing Company

www.crabtreebooks.com

Dedicated by Bobbie and Peter
For Tyler Brissenden,
Scott and Chelsea's adorable gift
to our huge, fun family.
Tyler is the 79th descendant!

Author and editor-in-chief
Bobbie Kalman

Publishing plan research and development
Reagan Miller

Editor
Kathy Middleton

Proofreader
Crystal Sikkens

Design
Bobbie Kalman
Katherine Berti
Samantha Crabtree (logo)

Photo research
Bobbie Kalman

Prepress technician
Samara Parent

Print and production coordinator
Margaret Amy Salter

Photographs
Thinkstock: page 13 (top right); bottom (ostrich chick)
Cover and all other images by Shutterstock

Library and Archives Canada Cataloguing in Publication

Kalman, Bobbie, author
        What kind of coverings do animals have? / Bobbie Kalman.

(All about animals close-up)
Includes index.
Issued in print and electronic formats.
ISBN 978-0-7787-1466-8 (bound).--ISBN 978-0-7787-1473-6 (pbk.).--
ISBN 978-1-4271-7638-7 (pdf).--ISBN 978-1-4271-7632-5 (html)

        1. Body covering (Anatomy)--Juvenile literature. I. Title.

QL941.K34 2015   j573.5   C2014-908182-0
                                                              C2014-908183-9

Library of Congress Cataloging-in-Publication Data

Kalman, Bobbie.
  What kinds of coverings do animals have? / Bobbie Kalman.
      pages cm. -- (All about animals close-up)
  Includes index.
  ISBN 978-0-7787-1466-8 (reinforced library binding : alk. paper) --
ISBN 978-0-7787-1473-6 (pbk. : alk. paper) --
ISBN 978-1-4271-7638-7 (electronic pdf : alk. paper) --
ISBN 978-1-4271-7632-5 (electronic html : alk. paper)
  1. Body covering (Anatomy)--Juvenile literature. I. Title.

QL942.K35 2015
591.47--dc23
                                        2014048906

Crabtree Publishing Company

www.crabtreebooks.com   1-800-387-7650

Printed in Canada/042015/BF20150203

Published in Canada
Crabtree Publishing
616 Welland Ave.
St. Catharines, Ontario
L2M 5V6

Published in the United States
Crabtree Publishing
PMB 59051
350 Fifth Avenue, 59th Floor
New York, New York 10118

Published in the United Kingdom
Crabtree Publishing
Maritime House
Basin Road North, Hove
BN41 1WR

Published in Australia
Crabtree Publishing
3 Charles Street
Coburg North
VIC 3058

Contents

What kinds of coverings?

This baby bonobo is covered in hair. Which animals have fur coverings? (See pages 6–9.)

People are mammals with hair. How else are they covered? (See pages 20–21.)

Animals have different kinds of coverings on their bodies. Their coverings suit their habitats, or the natural places where the animals live. **Mammal** bodies have hair or fur. **Reptile** bodies are covered with thin bony plates called scales. Turtles and tortoises are reptiles with hard shells. Birds are covered in feathers. Some animals have sharp spines, or spikes. Some have bodies that change.

Feathers help birds fly or move in other ways (see pages 12–13).

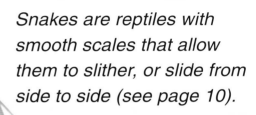

Snakes are reptiles with smooth scales that allow them to slither, or slide from side to side (see page 10).

Some animals have bodies and coverings that change (see pages 18–19).

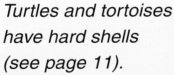

Turtles and tortoises have hard shells (see page 11).

This porcupine has sharp spines called quills (see pages 7, 14, and 15).

What do you think?

Which animals on this page are reptiles? Find four animals in this book that have spiny coverings like that of this porcupine.

Mammals have hair or fur

Most mammals have skin that is covered in hair or fur. Fur is soft, thick, short hair. Some ocean mammals have very little of either covering. Are the mammals on these pages covered with hair or fur? What other names do these coverings have? Find the answers on page 7.

cats

sheep

cheetah cubs

dog

hedgehog

Most cats are covered in fur, but some have no fur or hair, other than some **whiskers**.

Sheep are covered in soft, curly hair called wool.

Cheetah cubs have a mantle, or a covering of long fur, on their necks and backs. The mantle protects them from sun and rain and helps hide them in their grassy habitat.

Hedgehogs and porcupines have both hair and quills, which are made of keratin, like your nails.

Some dogs have short fur, and others have long hair. What is the covering on the dog shown on this page?

7

Thick fat and fur coats

polar bears

Some mammals live in places with very cold winters, and some live in cold oceans. Their bodies are protected from the cold by layers of fat called blubber. Some, like polar bears and arctic wolves, also grow thick fur.

The walruses below live in the freezing Arctic Ocean. They have thick layers of blubber covering their bodies. Other than whiskers, they have very little hair.

Arctic wolves have white fur year-round. White fur allows these wolves to blend in with their snowy habitat. In winter, they grow an extra layer of fur, which they shed in the spring. Their short, rounded ears help keep heat inside their bodies.

What do you think?

Arctic wolves and polar bears have white fur all year. Find an animal in this book whose fur is white only in winter.

Scales and shells

Snakes, lizards, turtles, and crocodiles are reptiles. Their bodies are covered with scales. Snakes have smooth scales, but other reptiles have rough scales called scutes. Some reptiles have shells.

crocodile

Alligators and crocodiles are covered in scutes.

Snakeskin is smooth.

leaf

gecko

tail

This leaf-tailed gecko's scutes look like tree bark, and its tail resembles a dying leaf. The gecko's covering hides it from animals that hunt and eat geckos.

Turtles and tortoises

Turtles and tortoises have shells. The outer layer of the shells is covered in scutes. Some turtles live in water, and some live on land.

Sea turtles live in oceans.

The shells of turtles and tortoises protect them. Many turtles can pull their bodies into their shells to keep from getting hurt.

tortoise

turtle

Tortoises have thick, strong shells that are very heavy. These reptiles live on land.

What do you think?

How do the coverings of leaf-tailed geckos and turtles protect them in different ways?

11

Fuzzy down and feathers

Baby birds are covered in down, or soft, fuzzy feathers. Down keeps them warm. Adult birds have down close to their bodies, but they are also covered with stiff feathers. These feathers give them their shape and color. Birds use these stiff feathers for flying, but not all birds can fly.

This adult parrot has long, stiff feathers on its wings, called flight feathers. Its tail feathers are very long, too.

These baby parrots have down feathers on their bodies and are starting to grow flight feathers.

down feathers

Ostriches cannot fly, but they are fast runners. Adult birds have four kinds of feathers that keep them warm or cool. Ostrich chicks, however, have only soft down feathers.

Penguins do not swim. They fly. Adult penguins have feathers that are close together to help keep water away from their skin. Penguin chicks are covered with soft, thin down.

King penguin chicks have brown down that they will shed. What colors will their new feathers be?

What do you think?

How do the feathers of each kind of bird help it move in a different way?

Coverings that scare!

Some coverings, such as sharp spines and bright colors, protect animals by scaring away predators. Predators are animals that hunt and eat other animals. Spines can be found on mammals, fish, and even insects.

Tenrecs are similar to hedgehogs and porcupines. They also have sharp spines.

Porcupinefish are able to make their bodies big and round by swallowing water or air. Their round shape and sharp spines make them look dangerous.

Don't eat me!

Bright colors and patterns warn that an animal may be **poisonous**. When predators see bright colors, they stay away!

When a fire-bellied toad sees a predator, it shows its bright red belly to scare it away.

eyespots

The bright green color on the saddleback caterpillar startles predators. Its spines contain poison that can cause pain.

The peacock butterfly's eyespots make this insect look much bigger than it is. The peacock caterpillar has a black spiny body. The sharp spines can cause pain when touched.

peacock caterpillar

Coverings that hide

Camouflage is colors and markings that allow animals to blend in with their surroundings. Some animals resemble parts of their habitat. This kind of camouflage is called mimicry. Animals that use mimicry are hard to spot because they look like parts of nature, such as flowers, leaves, or **coral**. Which animal on page 10 uses mimicry?

orchid mantis

orchid

The orchid mantis above blends in with the pink orchids on which it catches its prey, or the animals it hunts and eats.

Leaf insects look just like leaves. They even rock back and forth to mimic being blown by the wind.

The pygmy sea horse matches the pink bumpy coral around it. Can you tell where the sea horse is?

What do you think?

If you wanted to blend in with a forest, what color of clothes would you wear?

Coverings that change

Many animals have the same coverings for most of their lives, but some have coverings that change. Birds grow feathers, and some animals shed their coverings and grow new ones. For example, the fur of the snowshoe hare changes with the seasons.

The snowshoe hare's summer fur is brown.

In autumn, the fur starts changing color.

The hare's winter coat is white and much thicker.

Big changes

Some baby animals look like their parents. Other baby animals, such as frogs and butterflies, start out looking very different from their parents. Their bodies change two or more times before they become adults. This set of changes is called **metamorphosis**. Many insects go through metamorphosis.

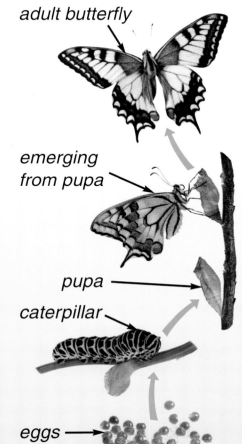

adult butterfly

emerging from pupa

pupa

caterpillar

eggs

What do you think?

A butterfly has wings. Describe how the coverings of caterpillars are very different from those of butterflies (also see pages 5 and 15).

Butterflies start their lives inside eggs laid by adults. A caterpillar hatches from each egg. Later, it creates a case around itself and becomes a pupa. It then emerges, or comes out, as a butterfly.

19

How are we covered?

People are mammals with hair. You cannot see some of our hair because we also cover our bodies in clothing. Unlike most animals, we can change the way we look by changing our hair or the clothes we wear. We change our clothes to suit the weather or the activities we do. We also wear certain clothes because we like how they look.

This girl wears different clothes to school than when she is exercising. How has she changed her hair?

Copycats!

We have copied many of our clothes from animal coverings. Some clothes help us do things that animals do, such as swim underwater in oceans.

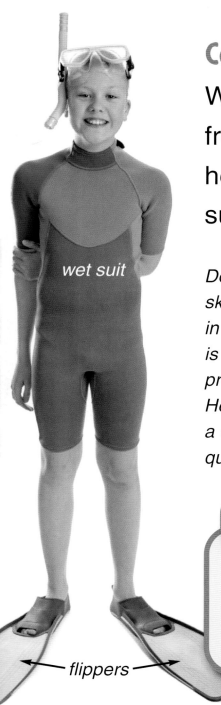

wet suit

flippers

Dolphins have thick skin, which protects them in the cold ocean. This boy is wearing a wet suit, which also protects his skin in the ocean. He is also wearing flippers like a dolphin's so he can swim quickly in ocean water.

flippers

What do you think?

Name five kinds of clothing you wear and describe why and where you wear each kind. Draw a picture of your favorite outfit and give reasons why you like it.

Match them up!

Which animals shown here match the coverings described in the box below?

Which animal...

1. *has a covering that changes as it grows?*
2. *has blubber under its thick, smooth skin?*
3. *has a covering that can cause pain to predators?*
4. *has a covering that changes with the seasons?*
5. *uses camouflage and mimicry to hide?*

Learning more

Books

Kalman, Bobbie. *What are nature's copycats?* (Big Science Ideas). Crabtree Publishing Company, 2012.

Kalman, Bobbie. *Animals grow and change* (Introducing Living Things). Crabtree Publishing Company, 2008.

Kalman, Bobbie. *Camouflage: Changing to Hide* (Nature's Changes). Crabtree Publishing Company, 2005.

Kalman, Bobbie and Kathryn Smithyman. *Metamorphosis: Changing Bodies* (Nature's Changes). Crabtree Publishing Company, 2005.

Rissman, Rebecca. *Comparing Body Coverings* (Body Coverings). Heinemann, 2009.

Websites

YouTube: Skin, Fur & Feathers (Animal Atlas)
www.youtube.com/watch?v=I_YnEGwxJj0

National Geographic: Find the Mimic
http://ngm.nationalgeographic.com/2009/08/mimicry/mimicry-interactive

eHow: Which animals have prickly spines?
www.ehow.com/info_8273105_animals-prickly-spines.html

Words to know

coral (KOR-uh-l) noun A small ocean animal that has a hard skeleton that supports it

mammal (MAM-uh-l) noun A warm-blooded animal that gives birth to live young

metamorphosis (met-uh-MAWR-fuh-sis) noun The big set of changes that some animals go through as they become adults

poisonous (POI-zuh-nuh-s) adjective Containing a harmful substance that causes pain, sickness, or death

reptile (REP-til) noun A cold-blooded animal that lays eggs

wet suit (wet soot) A tight-fitting rubber suit that keeps the bodies of swimmers warm in cold water

whiskers (WIS-kers) noun Long, stiff hairs growing around the mouths of certain animals and people

A noun is a person, place, or thing. An adjective is a word that tells you what something is like.

Index